TROLL
WILD ANIMALS

Library of Congress Cataloging-in-Publication Data

Dreyer, Ellen.
    Wild animals / by Ellen Dreyer, illustrated by Douglas Hall and
Graham Dennison.
        p.   cm.
    Summary: Describes a variety of wild animals and how they live in
their natural environments, including the leopard frog, snapping
turtle, opossum, and elephant.
    ISBN 0-8167-2242-0 (lib. bdg.)   ISBN 0-8167-2243-9 (pbk.)
    1. Animals—Juvenile literature.   [1. Animals.]   I. Hall,
Douglas, 1931-   ill.   II. Dennison, Graham, ill.   III. Title.
QL49.D74   1991
591—dc20
                                                    90-11163

Published in the U.S.A. by Troll Associates, Inc.,
100 Corporate Drive, Mahwah, New Jersey.
Produced by Joshua Morris Publishing Inc.
in association with Harper Collins.
Copyright © 1991 by Harper Collins.
Printed in Belgium.
10 9 8 7 6 5 4 3 2 1

TROLL
WILD ANIMALS

by
Ellen Dreyer
Illustrated by Douglas Hall
and Graham Dennison

Troll Associates

Introduction

Animals as we know them today are very different from animals as they first appeared millions of years ago. Indeed, the entire environment has changed drastically. The continents and oceans are in different places, and even the climate has made several extreme changes throughout the earth's history.

At one time, all life was in the sea. The land was completely barren, with no animals or plants. The oceans were filled with single-celled animals. Over time, more complex organisms made of many cells developed. They include sponges, jellyfishes, worms, and snails, as well as the ancestors of crabs, insects, and spiders. These are all *invertebrates*, or animals without backbones. Although there were no fishes, their ancestors – animals with the beginnings of a backbone – were also present. Later, fishes with fully developed backbones, or spinal columns, appeared. Animals with backbones are called *vertebrates*.

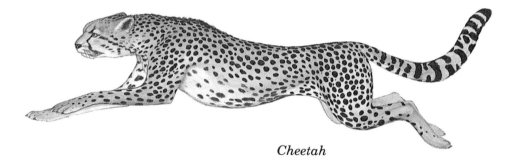

Cheetah

Fishes developed into many different shapes and forms. Some developed lungs, along with gills. This enabled them to breathe air directly, without having to depend on oxygen dissolved in the water. Other fishes gradually developed into *amphibians*, animals that could live both on land and in the water.

The amphibians, pioneers in a *terrestrial* (on-land) life, are the beginning of the story in this book. We will lead from them to the *reptiles*, and from those to the birds and mammals. Our emphasis will be on *mammals*, a group of vertebrates that includes human beings.

You may wonder why human beings belong to the mammal group instead of, say, the reptiles. Scientists have come up with a kind of filing system for placing different animals into groups with others. They choose animals that most closely resemble each other and put them together. This makes it easier to see the similarities and the differences.

This book will look mainly at wild animals, those animals that have not been tamed by human beings and that are not in our service. You will find out how vertebrates live and how they are specially suited to their own environments. Some of these are plant-eaters; others are flesh-eaters. Some live on the ground, while others live in trees. Still others live in the sea. You will discover which ones are most closely related.

Head of African elephant

Some live solitary lives, while others join together in herds. Some lay eggs, and some give birth to live young. Some are devoted parents, remaining with their offspring for long training periods. Others leave their offspring early in life. Some wander for long distances, while others remain in a small area all their lives. There are animals that forcefully hunt for prey. And there are animals that quietly take what is most easily available to them from the environment. You will find that there are definite reasons for each animal's lifestyle.

Amphibians

As more land and more food became available to them, the early amphibians began to prosper. They became more numerous and developed into many different *species*. (A species is a group of animals that have certain traits or characteristics in common.) Some became gigantic. They developed into fish-eaters, insect-eaters, or meat-eaters. Some lived on land all the time, while others lived only occasionally on land. But they all had to return to the water to have offspring. This was because their eggs were soft-shelled and could not survive on land. With no competition, the amphibians ruled the land.

One group of amphibians developed the ability to lay hard-shelled eggs. These eggs contained yolk to feed the developing young inside. Such eggs freed the vertebrates from a life in water. Now they could live and have offspring on land. The producers of these hard-shelled eggs were the reptiles. Reptiles quickly took over the amphibians' ruling position, and so the giant amphibians died out. Only smaller amphibians remained. Modern frogs, toads, and salamanders are the descendants of these animals.

Common toad

Salamander

The word *amphibian* means "having a double life." It is quite descriptive of the frogs, toads, and salamanders that belong to this group. These animals are able to live on land as well as in the water. Some remain in the water most of the time, while others live almost completely on land. Since all return to the water or to wet environments to produce offspring, the young look quite different from their parents. Their bodies are born equipped for life in the water. As they mature, they must change in order to live on land later.

Today's amphibians live in many different environments. There are toads and frogs living even in the desert, where they find small puddles when they are ready to produce offspring. Salamanders are found at sea level and on the tops of high mountains. Deep jungles provide homes for frogs not only on the ground but also up in the trees. The only continent on which no amphibian lives is Antarctica.

Common tree frog

Spotted tree frog

Amphibians have bodies ideally suited to their unusual lifestyle. Their skin, which has no scales, fur, or feathers, is kept moist by many glands. Water can pass through their skin in both directions while letting oxygen in and carbon dioxide out. This is important to the amphibian when on land, because its lungs are not as efficient at getting rid of waste gases as those of other kinds of animals. When the amphibian spends long periods underwater, its remarkable skin is even more important to breathing.

Amphibians shed their outermost layer of skin quite often. This is eaten by the animal as it is shed. Once its old skin is shed, the amphibian looks shiny in its new skin. But that is soon covered by dust and dirt, which serve as *camouflage* (a disguise or way of hiding).

Besides glands for keeping the skin moist, amphibians have many other kinds of skin glands. Tree frogs have glands in their toes that release a sticky substance enabling them to cling to trunks and branches. Other glands release substances that protect amphibians from their enemies, called *predators*. These substances irritate the eyes and mouths of other animals and sometimes cause nausea and paralysis in small species.

Although there are no large, dominant amphibians in today's environments, the many small species that have survived are highly successful animals.

Frogs and Toads

Frogs and toads have their eyes set at opposite sides of their heads, looking out in different directions. When something is nearby, they cannot focus on it. They are far-sighted, which works well for animals that eat flying insects. They can spot their dinner a long distance away and pick the right moment to leap. The location of their eyes is also useful in escaping from enemies, as they can see forward, backward, sideways, and upward at the same time.

Frogs and toads hear very well and make sounds to communicate with each other. Some can make sounds that can be heard for long distances. The sounds are usually produced by male frogs and toads calling to females when it is time to breed.

Frog eggs, laid in masses of several hundred or even several thousand, are attached to sticks and reeds in the water. Newly hatched frogs and toads are called tadpoles. They live in the water and have gills, a tail, and no legs. As they mature, they eventually change to resemble their parents.

Strawberry poison dart frog

Oriental fire-bellied toad

Leopard frog

Frogs and toads live mainly on insects and small animals such as spiders and worms, so their food supply is plentiful. Most toads have no teeth, and frogs usually have teeth only in their upper jaws. Most have an amazing tongue that fastens at the front instead of at the back of the mouth. The tongue is covered with a sticky substance. It pops out quickly to capture food, and the insect struck by the flicking tongue is hopelessly stuck.

Frogs and toads have very powerful hind legs that help them spring forward quickly.

The powerful hind leg of a frog helps it to leap.

Leopard Frog

The leopard frog is one of the most beautiful of all frogs. It lives in Canada and the United States. Most leopard frogs are shiny bronze, with soft yellow "leopard" spots on the back and head. The skin is smooth, and the body measures about three inches (about seven and a half centimeters).

Leopard frogs belong to the family that includes all the "true frogs." Other well-known members of the family are green frogs and bullfrogs. These are mostly slim-bodied, long-legged amphibians with pointed toes. "True frogs" do not burrow, nor do they escape their enemies by way of awful-smelling gland secretions. They use speed to escape. Leopard frogs are the best jumpers of the group. They can reach a distance of five feet (almost one and a half meters) in a single jump.

Leopard frogs hunt by day. Like most frogs, leopard frogs eat grasshoppers, spiders, beetles, and crickets.

Mature leopard frogs sleep through the winter in the muddy bottoms of ponds.

Horned Frog

Several different kinds of horned frogs are found in South America, the West Indies, the tropical United States, and Australia. They are very aggressive and will lunge at animals much larger than themselves. They have huge mouths and strong jaws. Their diet, however, consists of mainly beetles and earthworms.

The "horn" for which they are named is really just an extra flap of skin above each eye. This makes the head seem enormous. That seemingly large head, combined with the horned frog's aggressive behavior, is enough to frighten most predators away.

Some horned frogs reach a length of eight inches (about twenty centimeters), while other species are only about one inch (two and a half centimeters) long.

Arrow-Poison Frog

Deep in the forests of Central and South America lives a group of tiny frogs with a skin secretion so poisonous that they have become famous for it. Indians native to tropical America knew about this poison centuries ago. They used it to make poison-tipped arrows. The arrow, shot into a bird or small mammal, caused instant paralysis.

Horned frog

These little frogs – just one and a half inches (nearly four centimeters) in length – are beautiful. Some are black with shiny blue spots; others are green or pink with black spots. Some have bright yellow stripes. One, the golden arrow-poison frog of Central America, has a metallic bronze shine.

Red-eyed tree frog – Central America

Arrow-poison frog

Spring Peeper

The spring peeper is small – only one inch (two and a half centimeters) long – and drably colored in brown or gray. It has a special mark on it that makes it immediately recognizable: a small, black cross on its back. It belongs to the tree-frog family. The spring peeper can be found from Canada to Texas.

As you might guess, tree frogs live in trees and bushes. Their toes end in sticky disks, and their long legs help them to climb and cling. The spring peeper lives in woodlands near ponds or swamps. In early spring, the peepers can be heard in choral groups from bushes near the ponds. Their voice is a high-pitched whistle, repeated over and over. Their singing is one of the sounds of early spring.

American Toad

American toads belong to the family known as "true toads." "True toads" have fat bodies and short feet and are not very speedy travelers. To escape enemies, they rely on other characteristics. They are well camouflaged, blending in with their surroundings; the brown, warty skin looks just like the soil they sit upon. If threatened, some toads roll over on their backs and "play dead." Others burrow to safety. Toads also have a built-in weapon – glands on top of their head give off a poisonous fluid irritating to eyes and mouths.

Because their skin is thicker, toads can live farther away from water than frogs can. The body moisture of toads does not evaporate as quickly. As a result, toads are more likely than frogs to be seen in backyard gardens.

American toad

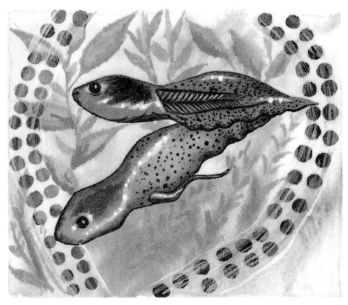

Toad tadpoles and eggs

The American toad of eastern North America is squat, with a big head. Females of this species grow up to be larger than males – up to four and a half inches (about eleven and a half centimeters) in length. Most are reddish-brown with a few spots of lighter brown. The warts on the head are often red or orange.

The eyes of a toad are very beautiful. The pupil is shiny black, and the iris is golden.

The female American toad lays tiny black eggs in long tubes of clear "jelly." The tubes are deposited at the bottom of a pond and take from five to twelve days to hatch. Each female lays up to 8,000 eggs in each tube. The young emerging from the eggs do not look at all like their parents. They are tiny tadpoles, more like fish with their gills and tails. As they mature, they develop legs and lose their tails. In about three to eight weeks, they resemble the parents. Thousands of these tiny toads fill the pond. They soon leave for the land, as their lungs have taken over the business of breathing. As they come on shore, they meet their enemies: snakes, hawks, and ducks.

The young toads that survive grow rapidly, shedding their skin when it gets too tight.

When a toad is ready for mating, it returns to the same pond in which it was hatched. Other toads are also there. Together the males begin to sing their pretty song of mating. The song is a sweet trill that seems to come from many directions at once and is irresistible to female toads.

The feeding place a toad establishes when still young remains its headquarters throughout life. Any cool, moist place makes a good home.

Giant Toad

This large "true toad" – nine inches (nearly twenty-three centimeters) long – lives throughout most of tropical North and South America. It can be found in Australia, the Philippines, and in the southern parts of Texas and Florida. Human beings have brought it into other warm areas because it is very valuable as a killer of insect pests. The large size of the giant toad allows it to eat many animals too big for other amphibians. In addition to insects, it eats small mammals such as mice.

Giant toad

Western Spadefoot Toad

This tiny toad is about one and a half inches (nearly four centimeters) long. It lives in the southwestern United States and Mexico. It gets its name from the sharp-edged warts shaped like spades (shovels) on its feet. These warts help the toad to burrow straight down into sandy or loose soil. It is dusky brown or gray in color, with scattered dark spots. These toads are at home in plains and dry environments. Spadefoot toads breed suddenly when there is rain in their area. Their eggs and tadpoles grow very quickly, so that little adult toads are ready to leave their temporary ponds before these dry out. The voice of the spadefoot is shrill; it sounds like a fingernail running along a comb.

The Surinam toad carries its eggs on its back.

Western spadefoot toad

Surinam Toad

The Surinam toad is one of a family of unusual amphibians without tongues. They are short, broad, and flat as a pancake. Surinam toads range in size from about four inches (about ten centimeters) to eight inches (twenty centimeters) in length. They are dark brown and have flaps of skin dangling from their jaws. This disguises the toads as they glide along the mud in their native rivers, the Amazon and the Orinoco, in South America.

The Surinam toad does not catch its prey in the usual toad way. It lives mainly in the water and sweeps its fingers through the mud at the bottom to uncover any small animals hidden there. Then, fanning the water around the prey, the toad swishes the meal into its gaping mouth.

Female Surinam toads have "pockets" on their backs for the carrying of eggs. After the male fertilizes the eggs, the pocket skin swells and covers over the eggs, making the mother look fat. The young remain in the pockets until after they have changed from tadpoles into tiny toads.

Surinam toad

Mexican Burrowing Toad

This tiny toad reaches only about two and a half inches (about six and a half centimeters) in length. It has a round body with a red or orange stripe down the middle of its back. When the Mexican burrowing toad calls out, its body becomes so inflated with air that it looks like a little balloon with a tiny, triangular snout sticking out. It remains in its burrow until heavy rains bring it out to breed.

Mexican burrowing toad

Surinam toad – completely transformed toadlets emerge and swim to the surface.

Reptiles

The early reptiles were the first to lay hard-shelled eggs with yolk inside for feeding the developing young. This breeding method fully equipped them for life on land and enabled them to inhabit many different kinds of environments. They dominated the earth. Dinosaurs ranging from chicken-size to whale-size roamed the earth, while huge marine reptiles ruled the waters. Strange-looking reptiles even flew overhead.

Eventually, one group of reptiles began to develop characteristics that would lead to a new group of animals – the birds. Another group developed into mammals. After millions of successful years, changes in the environment led to the destruction of most of these dominant reptiles. Modern reptiles consist only of the descendants of animals that survived the changes. These include turtles, alligators and crocodiles, lizards, and snakes.

Rainbow lizard

Double crested basilisk

Like amphibians, reptiles are cold-blooded. This means that they cannot keep their own body heat at a constant level. They get heat from the sun and can only control their temperature by moving to cooler or warmer places. But reptiles do not have smooth skin like amphibians. They have scales, shields, or plates. This kind of skin helps them live a completely terrestrial life by conserving water and protecting the animal from injuries. Like amphibians, snakes and lizards shed their skin. But unlike amphibians, snakes and lizards do not eat their shedded skin.

Turtles

Young reptiles, because they are born on land, do not have to go through a change in appearance. They look just like their parents when they hatch out of their eggs.

Reptiles are found in most parts of the world. They are particularly abundant in warm climates. In colder areas, they *hibernate* ("sleep" through the winter). There are reptiles in jungles, deserts, swamps, mountains, meadows, and even in oceans, although they breathe air.

The word *reptile* means "one that crawls or slithers." This, however, applies mostly to snakes. Most reptiles are good walkers and runners, although many of them move on sprawled-out limbs.

The body of a turtle is a remarkable thing. It has one of the most ideal defenses ever developed by an animal. The shell of a turtle protects the back and stomach completely. And usually there are holes in front and in back of the shell for the legs, tail, and head to retreat into whenever necessary. A turtle has no teeth, but its sharp beak makes it possible for it to eat fruit, vegetables, meat, or fish, depending on the turtle's diet. There are turtles living on land, in ponds and streams, and in the sea.

A turtle's shell is made up of two layers. The under layer, or *plastron*, is made of hard, bony plates. The outer layer, called a *carapace*, is

The giant tortoise lives in the Galapagos Islands, off the coast of South America.

covered with horny plates. The edges of the plates making up the two layers overlap, giving the armor great strength.

Sea, or marine, turtles live in warm waters all over the world, but they lay their eggs on land. Some sea turtles grow as large as 8 feet (more than 2 meters), reaching a weight of 1,500 pounds (675 kilograms). Because they cannot retreat into their shells, sea turtles must rely on their size and swimming ability for defense.

Sea turtle

Land turtles, frequently called tortoises, are usually smaller than marine turtles. However, the giant tortoises of the Galapagos Islands reach about 5 feet (1.5 meters) in length and weigh over 500 pounds (225 kilograms). Most of them, however, are small. One tiny tortoise weighs only about four pounds (about two kilograms).

Tortoises have thick, sturdy legs to support their bulk as they walk along the ground. Tortoises live in any area with a warm, even climate. Some also live in the desert, burrowing under the sand to escape the heat.

Common mud turtle

Most turtles live in ponds, streams, and marshy areas. These include snapping turtles, musk and mud turtles, cooters and sliders, and soft-shelled turtles.

There is a group of odd freshwater and marsh turtles, called side-necked turtles, that pull their heads in sideways. These live only in South America, Africa, and Australia.

The radiated tortoise lives in Madagascar.

Snapping Turtles

Snapping turtles are large, freshwater turtles with long tails. They are found from Canada to South America. The common snapper can grow to be about twenty inches (about fifty-one centimeters) long and weigh as much as thirty-five pounds (nearly sixteen kilograms). The alligator snapper grows to 30 inches (about 76 centimeters) and can weigh over 200 pounds (90 kilograms). Snapping turtles have large heads and relatively small shells. They also have knobby carapaces that are brown or black.

When they are in shallow water, snapping turtles often bury themselves in mud with only their eyes showing. They eat fish, reptiles, birds, and small mammals. They also eat plants.

Snapping turtle

Stinkpot (Common musk turtle)

The stinkpot is one of the musk turtles, a group that gets its name from an unpleasant odor given off from two glands on each side of the body. Musk turtles live in the water, crawling along the bottom. They leave the water only during heavy rain or when it is time to nest. They have small shells that offer little protection to the legs.

The stinkpot grows to about six inches (about fifteen centimeters) in length and lives in ponds, streams, and rivers from Canada to the Gulf of Mexico. There are two light stripes on its black head and *barbels* (little feelers made of skin) on its chin and throat. The carapace varies from light brown to black.

Head of snapping turtle

Stinkpot turtle

Red-Eared Slider Turtle

The red-eared slider turtle belongs to a group that includes cooters and sliders, turtles that enjoy lying in the sun for long periods. When the weather is not too hot or too cold, they come out of the water to lie on logs, stumps, or rocks. Sometimes, when space is limited, they pile up.

The red-eared slider gets its name from the red stripes in front of its ears.

The red-eared slider turtle reaches eight inches (about twenty centimeters) in length. It is recognizable by the broad red stripe behind its eyes. Red-eared slider turtles live in quiet waters with muddy bottoms throughout the central United States.

Smooth Soft-Shelled Turtle

The soft-shelled turtles, also called "softshells," are flat as pancakes. They are powerful swimmers and also can run on land with surprising speed. As the name suggests, the shell is soft-edged and leathery, without a horny layer. All softshells live in water. Most have a long nose, which they use as a breathing tube. Frequently, they lie buried in mud or sand in shallow water with only their eyes and nose showing. Members of this turtle family live in Africa, Asia, and North America.

Smooth soft-shelled turtle

The smooth soft-shelled turtle, sometimes called the "spineless softshell," lives in rivers or streams in the central United States. It is the only softshell without spines or bumps on the carapace.

Gopher Tortoise

Land turtles, or tortoises, are found on every continent except Australia and Antarctica. All tortoises have stumpy feet. Their hind feet look like those of elephants scaled down. The carapace of a tortoise is usually high and rounded. Tortoises feed mostly on plants.

The gopher tortoise of the southeastern United States has a smooth, brown carapace and a round head. It is an excellent burrower and makes tunnels as long as thirty-five feet (ten and a half meters) and wide enough for the turtle to turn around in. Other animals use the burrows as well. These include burrowing owls, raccoons, and opossums. Sometimes even rattlesnakes live there in peaceful harmony with the tortoise tunneler. Gopher tortoises feed on grass, leaves, and any wild fruit or berries they can find.

Green Turtle

Like all sea turtles, the green turtle is large, with flipperlike front feet. The Atlantic green turtle lives in the warm waters of the Gulf Stream and the Atlantic Ocean near North Carolina during the colder months. When the weather gets warmer, it moves up to New England, Nova Scotia, and Newfoundland.

The Atlantic green turtle reaches a length of 4 feet (more than 1 meter) and can weigh as much as 450 pounds (203 kilograms). Its color is brown. (The name *green turtle* comes from the greenish fat of its body.) Although the Atlantic

Green turtle emerging from its shell.

The green turtle comes ashore to lay her eggs on a sandy beach.

green turtle spends most of its life in the sea, it comes ashore to lay its eggs. When the young hatch, they go directly to the ocean.

Green turtles feed on marine plants, such as seaweed. But green turtles themselves are disappearing from the seas because of their popularity as food items.

The green turtle is a superb swimmer.

Crocodiles and Alligators

These reptiles are survivors of a group called *archosaurs* ("ruling reptiles") that also includes dinosaurs and the ancestors of birds. The strong, thick bodies and long, muscular tails of crocodiles and alligators help them live both on land and in water. When they swim, their tails move from side to side. Their strong legs carry their weight on land, allowing them to move quickly with the body raised well above the ground. Their heads are flat, and their teeth are sharp. Nostrils and eyes are at the top of their heads, so these animals can sense the world above them while staying mostly underwater.

Alligator young hatching

Alligators and crocodiles, as well as caimans (related to alligators) and gavials (related to crocodiles), are *carnivores* (meat-eaters). They feed on small animals found in the water and along the water's edge. Once the prey is caught, the crocodile sinks quickly to the bottom. In this manner, the tightly gripped prey is drowned, then torn apart and eaten.

American crocodile watching over eggs in grass

Crocodiles and alligators are the only reptiles that take care of their young. Eggs, laid in grass nests on shore, are carefully watched by the mother. When it is time for hatching, the mother may even help by breaking through the eggshell. Then, for at least a year afterward, the young are protected by their mothers from possible enemies in special nursery pools close to shore.

Black caiman

American Crocodile

There are crocodiles living in Africa, South America, and North America. The American crocodile ranges from the Gulf Coast to South America. It commonly reaches a length of twelve feet (three and a half meters) in the United States, but it can attain a length of twenty-three feet (seven meters) in South America. The coloring of crocodiles is grayish with darker markings.

American crocodile

Crocodiles often weigh less than alligators of the same length. But they are usually more active and aggressive than alligators. Crocodiles can move more quickly and have longer, more pointed snouts. An extra-long tooth on either side of the crocodile's lower jaw can still be seen when its mouth is shut. That same tooth in an alligator cannot be seen when its mouth is shut.

Male crocodiles make a low grumbling sound. Their sound is not as loud as the male alligators'.

American Alligator

Alligators are mostly distinguished from crocodiles by their broad, rounded snouts. The American alligator lives in swamps, marshes, and lakes in the southeastern United States. It can be as long as 12 feet (3½ meters) and weigh up to 550 pounds (247½ kilograms). It is usually gray or olive in color.

American alligator

The gavial (right) is a crocodile relative. It lives in India.

Male alligators roar. Females also roar, but not as loudly. The females also make grunting sounds when calling to the young. The young have a high-pitched moan, and alligators of all sizes can hiss.

Alligators make mounded nests of plants that can be as large as seven feet (about two meters) in diameter and three feet (nearly a meter) in height.

Alligators were considered an endangered species not long ago. Because of carefully enforced laws protecting them, they are now successfully increasing their numbers.

American alligator

Lizards

Lizards live mainly in the warmer regions of the world, although lizards can even be found in the cold areas above the Arctic Circle. They may live at sea level or as high as 16,000 feet (4,877 meters) up in the mountains. There are about 3,000 different species, or kinds, of lizards.

Unlike snakes, lizards have ear openings on the sides of their heads and movable eyelids so they can close their eyes. Some have forked tongues, like snakes, but most have thick, fleshy tongues. One kind of lizard, the chameleon, has a tongue as long as its body. The tongue shoots out almost faster than the human eye can see. Some chameleons have a tongue covered with a sticky substance. This makes the tongue a valuable hunting weapon, snaring not only insects but also birds and other reptiles.

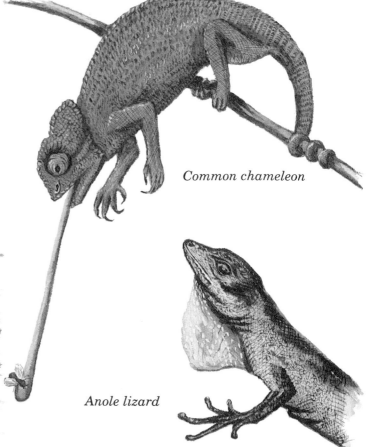

Common chameleon

Anole lizard

There is an amazing variety of lizards. They come in all sizes. Most are small, but there are also giant lizards, such as the Komodo dragon.

Komodo Dragon

This giant, which can grow up to ten feet (three meters) long, is the largest living lizard. The Komodo dragon belongs to a group of lizards known as *monitors*. They live in Africa, Australia, and India. Some other monitors can grow up to seven feet (about two meters) in length. Monitors have forked tongues and other features resembling those of snakes.

The Komodo dragon lives on the islands of southeast Asia. It stalks and kills deer and also feeds on dead animals.

Anoles

Anoles (uh-NOH-lees) are lizards found throughout North and South America, but most live in the tropics. All of them bob their heads and do "pushups" to appear aggressive and angry when they are announcing their territorial rights.

There are 300 anole species. This is the largest individual group of reptiles in the Western Hemisphere. They are especially abundant in the tropics. One species, the green anole, is native to the United States. Male anoles have a brightly colored throat flap, called a dewlap. It can be flared out when they are trying to attract females or scare away other males.

Knight anole

Komodo dragon

Anoles can change color quickly to blend in with their surroundings. They can be brown, gray, or green. They have sticky pads on their feet that assist them in climbing. Their food consists mainly of insects and spiders.

Green anole

Green anoles can reach eight inches (about twenty centimeters) in length. They are often seen in the southern United States, sitting on fences or against buildings.

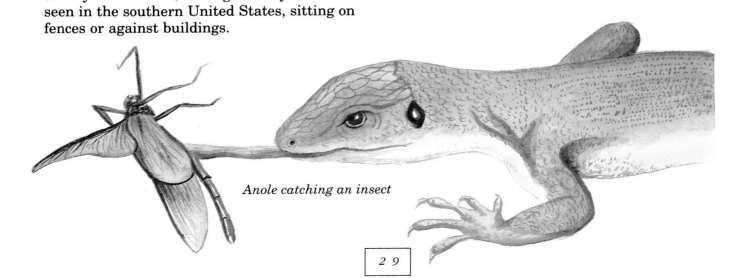

Anole catching an insect

Snakes

There are about 2,700 species of snakes, inhabiting almost as many places as the lizards. They can be found on every continent except Antarctica.

Instead of legs, snakes have special scales on their bellies to assist them in moving. These work very well, and one can find snakes up in the trees, moving rapidly along the ground, or swimming. Snakes can even be found underground. Special hinges in a snake's jaw allow it to be opened very wide for the swallowing of prey. All snakes are meat-eaters. They are excellent hunters, although they have poor eyesight and limited hearing ability. They have an excellent sense of smell, however. Snakes pick up scents with their forked tongues as they move along. Poisonous snakes have fangs and *venom*, or poison, glands. They bite their victims, then inject a shot of venom.

Emerald boa

Python

Garter Snakes

Garter snakes are slender, nonpoisonous snakes with brightly colored stripes running down their sides. They reach about twenty-four inches (sixty centimeters) in length. The eastern garter snake lives in meadows, woodlands, and along the edges of streams in North America from eastern Canada to New England.

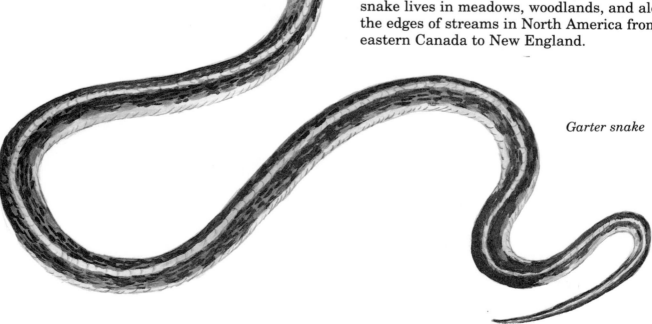

Garter snake

Pit Vipers

Among the poisonous snakes, those most familiar to people in North America are the pit vipers. These include copperheads, cottonmouths, and rattlesnakes. The name *pit viper* comes from the deep pit found on each side of the snake's face, midway between the eye and the nostril. It is a temperature-sensitive organ that helps the snake to aim when striking at warm-blooded prey. All pit vipers are poisonous. Pit vipers can be found everywhere except Antarctica and Australia. Rattlesnakes are restricted to North and South America. They have been divided into thirty-one species. Rattlesnakes, or "rattlers," are best known for the "rattles" on the tips of their tails. These are loosely attached horny rings that hit against each other, making a buzzing sound whenever the tail is shaken. A young rattler has only a single ring on its tail, but each time it sheds its skin, a new ring is made. Adult rattlers usually have eight rings.

Most rattlesnakes would rather slip away when a human being approaches. But if you should hear the warning rattle, you would be wise to move in another direction.

The eight rings at the end of a typical rattlesnake's tail

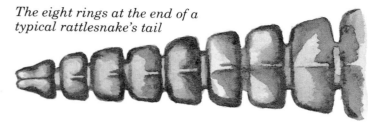

Boas and Pythons

Boas and pythons are more primitive than other snakes in that their bodies have changed less from those of the earliest known snakes. The males have tiny hind legs shaped like spurs on their underside. These are not used for walking, but for mating.

American rattlesnake

Different species of rattlesnakes produce different kinds of rattling noises. Usually, the largest snakes are the loudest. They feed mostly on rodents and birds, but they also eat frogs and lizards.

Cottonmouth

This snake family includes some giants among snakes. Species that climb have a *prehensile* tail, which means it is muscled for hanging on to branches. None of these snakes are poisonous. They kill their prey through *constriction*. The victim is seized with the teeth, then the snake coils its body around it. It uses its powerful muscles to squeeze, or constrict, its victim. Every time the victim takes a breath and lets out air, the snake squeezes more tightly. Finally, breathing is no longer possible and the victim dies. Then, the snake swallows it whole.

There are about fifty-four different species of boas. They live mostly in Central and South America, but some are found in Asia, Africa, and North America. Boas bear live young, while pythons hatch from eggs.

Anaconda

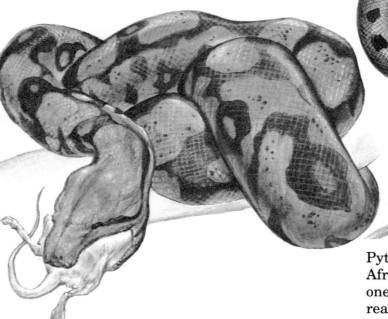

A boa constrictor can swallow a rat whole.

Pythons are mainly found in tropical Asia, Africa and Australia. The reticulate python is one of the largest snakes in the world. It can reach a length of thirty feet (nine meters). When a female python lays her eggs, she *incubates*, or warms, them by coiling around the heap of eggs and staying with them until they hatch. Hatching usually takes place in about eighty days.

Birds

Although birds are now separated into a class of their own and certainly look quite different from reptiles, they are descendants of reptiles. During the time when the earth was ruled by reptiles, some of the archosaurs (the group that includes crocodiles and dinosaurs) developed into flying, feathered animals. If you were to strip off the feathers, a bird's body is very similar to that of a small dinosaur. Scientists think that birds are closely related to the dinosaurs. They either come from the same ancestors or are descended from dinosaurs themselves.

There are about 8,600 different species of birds in the world. Over 700 species are in North America alone. Some of these are swimmers, very much at home in the water. Others cannot fly and can only live on the ground. But the majority are good flyers and often perch in trees. Most of the smaller birds are seed-eating and/or insect-eating songbirds. Larger species include fish-eating gulls and cormorants. For many people, however, the most fascinating birds are the birds of prey. These include owls, eagles, hawks, ospreys, and vultures.

Hummingbird

Flamingo

Birds are warm-blooded, meaning that their bodies can maintain a constant temperature regardless of the weather. All birds reproduce by laying eggs, and they are devoted parents. They are social animals, frequently living in groups. They even fly together over long distances from their nesting grounds to their winter homes. Most birds go through elaborate courtship rituals to determine pairing during the breeding season. Some birds stay with one mate all their life.

Owls

Owls are night hunters, with keen sight for seeing at night and keen hearing and smell for locating small prey hidden in the darkness. Their fluffy feathers silence their flight so that they are almost soundless when hunting. Owls eat a variety of meat, but they specialize in rodents.

Barn owl with young

Great horned owl

Owls range in size from that of a sparrow to that of an eagle. They are found worldwide. There are species of owls living in the Arctic tundra and tropical grasslands. There are also owls living in the desert. Some owls make underground burrows, but most perch in trees.

Great Horned Owl

The great horned owl, which reaches a length of about twenty-two inches (about fifty-six centimeters), is one of the largest owls. It gets its name from its long ear tufts, which give the appearance of horns. The great horned owl's homes include forests, cities, and deserts throughout North and South America. It is a fierce hunter, with its large claws, and pursues such animals as skunks and grouse. The call of a great horned owl is a series of deep, loud hoots.

Barred Owl

The barred owl, which is almost as large as the great horned owl, is chunky and has dark eyes. It lives in woods, frequently near rivers or swamps. The call of the barred owl is very distinct: a series of eight or more hoots ending with an "ah." It lives in the eastern part of North America.

Northern Saw-Whet Owl

The tiny saw-whet owl reaches only eight inches (about twenty centimeters) in length. Saw-whets live in forests and swamps from Alaska to Mexico. Its primary call, which is heard mostly in the breeding season, is a single whistled note repeated over and over. It is named, however, for another call it makes, a rasping noise that sounds like a saw being sharpened, or whetted.

Common Barn Owl

This pale owl, which reaches a length of eighteen inches (about forty-six centimeters), has dark eyes in a white, heart-shaped face. It roosts and nests in dark holes in city and farm buildings, on cliffs, and in trees. Its call is a raspy screech or hiss.

Common barn owl

Saw-whet owl

Eagles and Hawks

Eagles and hawks are birds of prey. They hunt by day, using their keen sight to locate prey from great distances. They have hooked bills and strong hooked claws, called talons. They range in size from the huge, soaring bald eagle that is thirty-five inches (ninety centimeters) in length to the slim sharp-shinned hawk that is often no more than ten inches (about twenty-five centimeters) in length. Eagles and hawks are found on every continent except Antarctica.

Golden Eagle

The golden eagle, which can be found from Canada to Mexico as well as in Asia and Europe, reaches a length of thirty-five inches (ninety centimeters). It has a wingspan of more than seven feet (two meters). Golden eagles are brown with gold on the back of the head and neck. They live in mountainous or hilly areas where they can be seen soaring with their wings spread. They hunt over open country for rodents, snakes, and other birds.

Bald eagle

Golden eagle

Bald Eagle

The bald eagle, the national bird of the United States, is seen frequently in Alaska. Throughout the rest of the United States and Canada, it may be found in small numbers on seacoasts or near rivers and lakes. This is because bald eagles feed mainly on fish as well as dead or dying animals. Bald eagles reach thirty-five inches (ninety centimeters) in length, with a wingspan of eight feet (about three meters). They are not bald, but have white feathers on their head and tail, while the rest of their body is brown. They have huge yellow beaks. Bald eagles nest in tall trees or on cliffs. These handsome birds are endangered from overhunting and from taking in pesticides.

Red-Tailed Hawk

The red-tailed hawk, seen throughout North and Central America and the West Indies, does have a red tail when it becomes fully mature. It is up to twenty-five inches (about sixty-four centimeters) long, with a wingspan of about four feet (more than one meter). Red-tailed hawks frequently live in wooded areas near open land, but they can also be seen on the plains and even over the desert. They feed mostly on rodents.

Osprey

Red-tailed hawk

Northern Goshawk

The northern goshawk is found throughout Canada and in the northern United States. A fierce hunter, it lives in deep woods. There it makes surprise attacks on ground birds, although it may also catch mammals as large as rabbits. The northern goshawk reaches a length of twenty-six inches (sixty-six centimeters).

Osprey

The osprey is often thought to belong to the same bird family as eagles and hawks. But most ornithologists (people who study birds) have put ospreys into their own group. The osprey is found on all the continents of the world except Antarctica. It lives near rivers, lakes, or seacoasts. When hunting for fish, ospreys fly over the water, diving feet first to grip their prey. They build bulky nests in trees, on buildings, or on docks. At one time, they were endangered by the use of pesticides, but recently they have recovered. Ospreys reach a length of twenty-four inches (sixty-one centimeters).

Falcons

Found worldwide, falcons have longer, narrower wings than hawks. Falcons include the smallest of the birds of prey – tiny falcons only six inches (fifteen centimeters) long that prey on insects. But other falcons feed on a variety of larger prey as well as carrion (the flesh of dead animals). They are powerful hunters.

American Kestrel

The American kestrel is a deadly hunter that, like all falcons, can be distinguished from hawks by its long, pointed wings bent back at the "wrists." The American kestrel, which lives throughout Canada, the United States, and Mexico, reaches up to fifteen inches (thirty-eight centimeters) in length. It has a wingspan of about two feet (one-half meter). It has a reddish back and tail and a white face with black stripes. Found in open country and cities, the kestrel feeds on insects and small rodents. These birds are often seen perching on telephone wires. The American kestrel is sometimes called the American sparrow hawk.

American kestrel

Peregrine Falcon

Except in polar regions, peregrine falcons used to be found worldwide. But they have become rare in recent years because of the use of pesticides. Peregrine falcons live on cliffs and near open wetlands. They prey mainly on ducks, shore birds, and sea birds. Peregrines reach a length of eighteen inches (about forty-six centimeters).

New World Vultures

The family of New World vultures lives throughout North and South America. They mostly eat carrion, the meat of dead animals, which is easier to tear with their beaks and claws. Vultures have small, usually unfeathered heads. They do not build nests, but instead lay their eggs in a sheltered spot, such as a cave or a hollow log. Flocks often roost together.

Turkey vulture

Peregrine falcon

Turkey Vulture

The turkey vulture belongs to the New World family, a separate group from Old World vultures. Turkey vultures are found from southern Canada to Argentina. They prefer dry, open country and woodlands. The turkey vulture rarely flaps its wings in flight, but does rock from side to side. Flying and gliding for long periods, it searches for carrion and garbage. It reaches a length of thirty inches (seventy-six centimeters).

California Condor

This large bird, also a New World vulture, can grow as long as four and a half feet (about a meter and a half). The California condor also has a wingspread of up to nine and a half feet (nearly three meters). Until recently, it was found in the foothills and mountains of southern California. But the California condor has become almost extinct because of overhunting and eating poisoned animals. There are now a few in captivity, where people are trying to breed them in an effort to return them to the wild. Condors feed on the carrion of large animals, such as deer, cattle, and sheep.

The California condor is almost extinct.

Old World Vultures

The family of Old World vultures lives in Europe, Asia, and Africa. Among Old World vulture species are the cinereous, or European black, vulture; the lammergeier, or bearded vulture; and the Egyptian vulture. A bully, the cinereous vulture often swoops in and forces off other vultures feeding on carrion. The lammergeier sometimes feeds on the marrow inside animal bones, which it breaks open by dropping them on rocks from high above. The Egyptian vulture likes to eat ostrich eggs. To break an egg open, this vulture picks up a small rock with its beak and drops it on the shell.

Mammals

Along with the ruling reptiles of prehistoric times was a group with characteristics that would lead to the development of mammals. These animals are called "mammal-like reptiles." They were spread throughout the world. They began as hairless, egg-laying, cold-blooded reptiles. But they developed more and more mammalian traits, gradually becoming as much mammal as reptile. Their legs were pushed under the body, with the elbows bent backward and the knees forward, making them good runners. Their teeth became better equipped for slicing and grinding up food. Being able to cut food into tinier pieces led to better

Grizzly bear

digestion and a more energetic kind of living. These final steps of development marked the very beginning of the mammals we know today.

Small insect-eating and plant-eating mammals were living in the time of the dinosaurs, but their role was a minor one. Not until the dinosaurs became extinct did the mammals begin to spread out and grow in size and variety. Mammals then took over all the important roles on land that the dinosaurs before them had held.

You are a mammal. So are camels, whales, dogs, rabbits, porcupines, and platypuses. There are some noticeable differences among mammals, but there are also common characteristics that relate to all of us.

Cheetah

All mammals have hair or fur covering them. Mammal mothers of every type feed milk from their own bodies to their young. Mammals are vertebrates, which means they have a backbone. Of particular importance is the mammal's large brain, which usually means greater intelligence. Mammals also have very efficient teeth, separated into incisors for nipping, canines for slicing, and molars for grinding. And all mammals are able to keep a constant body temperature because they are warm-blooded animals.

Short-beaked echidna

Platypus diving

Monotremes

There is a very strange group of mammals called *monotremes*. This group includes the duck-billed platypus and echidnas (ih-KIHD-nuhs), also called spiny anteaters. These unusual animals, which seem to be half-mammal and half-reptile, live in Australia, Tasmania, and New Guinea.

At first glance, the monotremes seem like ordinary mammals, for they have hair and mammary glands. They are also warm-blooded. Certain parts of the skeleton, however, are more like those of reptiles than of mammals. What is really strange is that, unlike all other mammals, the female monotreme lays eggs. The eggs have leathery shells like those of reptiles. Monotremes are warm-blooded, but their body temperature is lower than that of most mammals and varies in extreme weather.

Long-beaked echidna

Scientists believe that monotremes are a separate line of mammals that arose directly from some of the mammal-like reptiles.

Platypus

The platypus lives in the streams and lakes of eastern Australia and Tasmania. The males are bigger and heavier than the females, reaching about eighteen inches (nearly forty-six centimeters) in length and weighing about four pounds (about two kilograms). Platypus hair is velvety and smooth, and the body is slender. The paddle-shaped tail serves as a rudder in diving and surfacing. The legs are short and stout, and the feet are webbed. Instead of a snout, there is a bill of naked, leathery skin. The nostrils open at the top of the bill.

Young platypuses have small teeth that later fall out. Adults have hornlike plates along the jaw.

When on land, the platypus can see and hear well. But when submerged in water, it is blind and deaf, for the eyes and ears are covered by folds of skin. The webs of the front feet, which are useful in swimming, can be folded back under the palms when walking on land.

The female builds a special burrow along the stream bank to use as a nest. Into this burrow she carries wet leaves to provide moisture for her eggs. The burrow is then plugged up with earth. The young hatch in about ten days. The mother stays in the burrow for days at a time to nurse the young, which feed by licking milk from glands on her belly. When the mother does leave, she removes and rebuilds the plug. After about four months, the young are mature enough to leave the burrow.

Platypuses use their bills to search for food on the bottoms of streams. They eat crayfish, snails, tadpoles, and insect larvae.

Duck-billed platypus and young

Marsupials

Marsupial mammals are different from other mammals in several ways. First of all, most females have a *marsupium*, or pouch. Marsupial young are born at a very early stage of development, and the pouch is a sort of built-in incubator. The babies are just barely able to claw their way up to the mother's pouch, where they stay attached to her nipples, fed and protected, for several months.

Another important difference is the size of the brain case. The marsupial's is considerably smaller, making it less intelligent than other mammals.

At one time, marsupials lived side by side with other mammals throughout the world. As the two groups progressed, the marsupials began to lose ground. They became restricted to the continents of South America and Australia.

At one time, there were many different kinds of marsupials in South America, but only opossums and opossum rats survived. They are still thriving in South America, and opossums have made their way to North America as well.

Australia is the home of a large variety of marsupials. Modern Australian marsupials include grazers, browsers, fruit-eaters, and meat-eaters. They include such groups as kangaroos, koalas, phalangers, and native "cats."

Scaly-tailed opossum

Numbat

Squirrel glider

Opossums

Many opossums, which are marsupials, are covered with coarse, gray hair, except on the tail, which is naked. The tail is prehensile, which means that it is very muscular and can be used for hanging on to things like the branches of trees. Opossums have clawed toes on their feet. With such feet and tails, opossums are great climbers and feel quite comfortable moving around in trees.

There are numerous species of opossums living in South America, but only one species, the common opossum, is found in North America as well. This species lives in all kinds of environments. The body is about eighteen inches (about forty-six centimeters) long, with a tail that is longer than the body. The big toe is large, clawless, and *opposable*, meaning that it is set off to the side so the opossum can grasp objects. Opossums have small, sharp teeth and pointed snouts. The common opossum ranges from southern Canada, through the United States and Mexico, and all the way down to Argentina.

Yapok opossum

Opossum and young

Opossums are active during the evening and at night. They are mostly *arboreal*, which means they live in trees. They eat insects, small rodents, fruit, berries, and carrion.

When an opossum is frightened, it may "play possum." It pretends to be dead to discourage enemies from attacking. Actually, it lies on its side with its tail rolled up and with its eyes and mouth gaping.

As with most marsupial babies, common opossums are born at a very early stage of development and continue to mature within the mother's pouch. After leaving the pouch about two months later, the young travel on the mother's back, clinging to her fur.

Koalas

Koalas live in the eucalyptus forests of Australia. There is only one species. They are about thirty inches (seventy-six centimeters) long and have no tail. The thick, woolly fur is grayish. The koala's big head, hairy ears, and large nose make them appealing animals.

Koalas are completely arboreal, rarely leaving the eucalyptus trees where they live and feed. They are gentle animals who live either singly or in groups. An adult male usually has a number of females that he guards. A single offspring, called a cub, is born to each female. It remains in its mother's pouch for about six months, then rides on her back for another six months.

Koala

Koala and young

Kangaroos

There are fifty-two species of kangaroos in Australia, Tasmania, and New Guinea. They vary in size from only nine inches (twenty-three centimeters) in length to more than five feet (one and a half meters). Larger kangaroos may stand over six and a half feet (two meters) in height. In all, the head is small in relation to the body, and the ears are large. The hairy tail is long and thick at the base. It is used as a prop when standing and as a balancing organ when the animal is leaping. The hind legs are large and strong, while the forelegs are small. The female has a well-developed pouch for carrying her young.

Kangaroos have teeth that are ideal for grazing or browsing. They eat almost every kind of plant matter. Most kangaroos are active at night, spending the day in grassy nests or shallow burrows. They like to sunbathe on warm afternoons.

Kangaroos can leap great distances.

Kangaroo and young, called a joey

Insectivores

At the same time that the first marsupials were beginning to develop, toward the end of the Age of Dinosaurs, another group of mammals, the *placentals*, also had their beginnings. These mammals can grow an organ, called a *placenta*, inside the mother's body. The placenta provides food for developing babies. In this way, placental babies are at a much more complete stage of development at birth than marsupial babies.

The first placental mammals belonged to a group called *insectivores*, since these animals fed mostly on insects and other small invertebrates. None of them became very large. One insectivore family, the shrews, includes the smallest of all living mammals. Probably the small size and secretive ways of the insectivores have helped make them so successful for so long.

47

Ancient insectivores are thought to be the ancestors of all the other types of placental mammals, such as bats, primates, carnivores, hoofed mammals, and elephants.

Modern insectivores include shrews, moles, hedgehogs, and the odd, spiny tenrecs of Madagascar. North American insectivores include only moles and shrews.

Moles

Shrew

Pygmy shrew

Moles

Moles live in Europe, Asia, and North America. Some species burrow in stream banks on occasion, but most spend their entire lives underground. The common mole of North America is about eight inches (twenty centimeters) long. Most species construct two types of burrows: one very deep in the ground for shelter and care of their young; the other, a shallow burrow for resting and feeding.

Moles have eyes that are hidden in their fur. They are almost blind. They have good hearing, however, although their ears are not visible. Moles have beautiful, glossy fur.

Shrews

Shrews are found in almost every part of the world. They are small, mouselike animals with long, pointed snouts. The smallest mammal in the world is a pygmy shrew about one inch (two and a half centimeters) long, weighing less than one ounce (twenty-eight grams).

Most shrews live on the ground, but some burrow a little and some like to swim. Shrews are quick-moving and nervous.

Bats

Bats are very closely related to the insectivores. They are the only mammals that can fly. Bat wings are formed of extensions of the skin of the back and belly, and they are attached to the arms, legs, and tail. The entire hand is involved in supporting the wing, except for the thumb, which is free for clutching. The hind legs, which are used for hanging when the bat sleeps, are very weak and cannot support the animal on the ground.

Because most bats are *nocturnal*, or active at night, they have highly developed hearing. They are able to sense the presence of nearby insects in the dark. Some eat things other than insects. There are fruit-eating bats, which have faces like foxes'. There are fish-eating bats, which use hooked claws on the back feet for catching fish. Flower-eating bats have long tongues with brushlike tips for sucking up pollen and nectar. Blood-sucking bats have sharp incisors for making cuts in their victims.

Little Brown Bats

There are sixty species of little brown bats found throughout the world, except for the Arctic and Antarctic. They range in size from about one and a half inches (about three and a half centimeters) to three inches (nearly eight

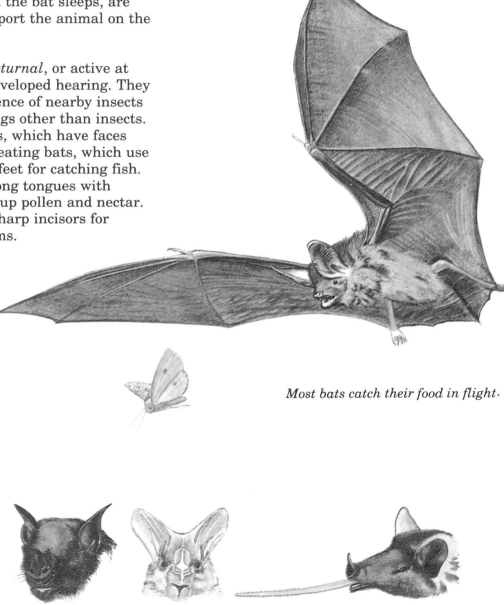

Most bats catch their food in flight.

Bats hang upside-down to sleep.

Bat heads show a great variety of differences between species.

centimeters) in body length. Some live in the woods, while others are more common in open areas. Many live in caves, attics, and towers. Most of them enjoy living in large groups.

Females usually form large colonies for rearing their young. There may be as many as 10,000 in such a colony. Births occur in the spring and summer, with usually one offspring per mother.

Little brown bats feed on insects. Their feeding flights usually are interrupted by periods of rest, during which the bat hangs upside down to digest its catch.

The horseshoe bat is named for the shape of the growth on its nose.

Greater horseshoe bat *Lesser horseshoe bat*

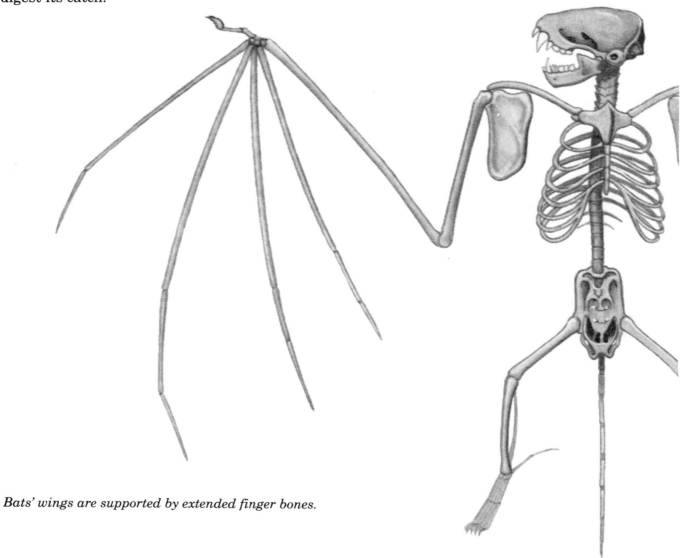

Bats' wings are supported by extended finger bones.

Primates

Primates broke off from the insectivores at a very early time in the history of mammals. Other groups that appeared early from the same ancestry are the carnivores and the rodents, making these groups more closely related to primates than to other mammals. As each order broke away from the insectivores, it developed its own unique ways of living and feeding.

An interesting thing about the way primates developed is that they underwent fewer body changes than other kinds of mammals. In many ways, primates remained similar to their ancestors. They have not developed horns, trunks, or hooves. The simple structure of the primates has given them the advantage of great flexibility.

Like many of the earliest mammals, primates began as tree-living animals. Most primates continued this way of life throughout their history. Because they were up high, their eyesight became more important to them than the sense of smell. Binocular vision (using both eyes together) is more highly developed in primates than in other mammals, and the eyes are directed forward rather than to the sides. The size of the nose is smaller, as is the portion of the brain connected to the sense of smell. The thinking part of the brain is very large. The hands are flexible, with an opposable thumb for easy grasping. Good eyesight, the use of the hands, and a keen intelligence are the factors that led to the success of the primates.

Lesser Senegal bush baby

Nocturnal slender loris

Tree Shrews

The first primates were creatures much like the modern tree shrews. There are five types of tree shrews, all living in the forests of eastern Asia. Tree shrews look like long-snouted squirrels. Their feet are hairless, with padded soles and long, flexible toes.

Tree shrew

Tree shrews are active little animals that climb well and run swiftly. They are constantly searching for food – anything from insects to fruit and worms.

Fat-tailed dwarf lemur

Lemurs

From animals like the tree shrews, the primates went on to develop into lemurlike animals. Modern lemurs live only on the islands of Madagascar and Comoros, off the coast of Africa. There are several kinds of lemurs, ranging from mouse size to fox size. They all have long, furry tails.

The mouse lemur is only about five inches (almost thirteen centimeters) long, with a round head and a short snout. Its eyes and ears are large. It sleeps through the hottest weather.

White verreaxs sifaka lemur

The indri, at twenty-eight inches (seventy-one centimeters), is the largest lemur. Long, soft fur covers its body, but its face, hands, and feet are naked. The eyes are large, and the nose is short. Indris live in family groups in trees. When they do come to the ground, they stand erect and move in jumps, holding their hands above their heads.

Lorises

The lorises are close relatives of the lemurs. The noses of the lorises are smaller than those of the lemurs, and their eyes are placed farther forward. Most lorises are about ten inches (about twenty-five centimeters) long. They have no tails. There are six types of lorises living in the forested areas of Africa and Asia. These creatures feed on insects, fruit, young birds, and bird eggs.

The slow loris gets its name from the careful way in which it moves. It is active only at night, spending the day rolled up in a ball in a hollow tree. It sometimes hangs head downward, hanging on by its feet.

Tarsiers

There are three species of tarsiers (TAHR-see-uhrs), all of which live in the East Indies and the Philippines. These are little animals, reaching a length of no more than six inches (fifteen centimeters).

The outstanding feature of the tarsier is its enormous eyes. Located in the middle of its face and set very close together, the eyes leave almost no room for the tiny nose. The tarsier also has big, thin, hairless ears. Its forelegs are short, but the hind legs are quite long. That makes the tarsier a good jumper. Unlike the loris, the tarsier has a tail. The pads on its toes and fingers help it hold on tightly to tree limbs.

Tarsiers can turn their heads nearly all the way around. They can see in every direction. Tarsiers are great acrobats, hopping long distances from branch to branch. On the ground, they are able to walk on all fours, but usually they leap like frogs.

Night feeders, tarsiers like to eat snails, small lizards, and insects.

Tarsier

Monkeys

There are two separate groups of monkeys, New World (found in Central and South America) and Old World (found in Asia and Africa). Both groups arose at about the same time from tarsier ancestors. They both have large, forward-facing eyes, a larger brain case than that of tarsiers and lemurs, and better hand development.

The nostrils of New World monkeys are widely separated, while in Old World monkeys they are closer together.

Face of Old World monkey   *Face of New World monkey*

New World Monkeys

Some of the New World monkeys have a prehensile, or grasping, tail, but none of the Old World monkeys do. There are two groups of New World monkeys. The first group, which includes various species of spider monkeys, howler monkeys, and capuchins, lives in tropical forests from Mexico to Argentina. The second group includes just marmosets and tamarins. All New World monkeys are arboreal, meaning they live in trees.

Night or owl monkey

Dusky titi monkey

Red uakari

Howler Monkeys

The howler monkeys, or howlers, reach a length of two feet (sixty-one centimeters), excluding the tail. The tail is prehensile in four of the species, who use it as an extra hand for grasping objects or in climbing. Howler monkeys are the largest of the New World group. Their fur is long and coarse, and their faces are bare. Their voices are very loud and have been compared to the roar of lions.

Howler monkeys live in large groups and travel through the trees, making a great noise, which can carry for two miles (about three kilometers) through the jungle.

Spider Monkeys

Spider monkeys have very long arms and legs, which give them their name. Their prehensile tails are flexible, but their thumbs are poorly developed for grasping. They move about quickly in trees and are able to hang by a single hand or foot.

Capuchin Monkeys

Capuchin (KAP-yuh-chihn) monkeys live in the very tops of the tallest trees and rarely come down to the ground. They are sociable, living in groups of from five to thirty, and chatter to each other for hours. Capuchins grow to about

Howler monkey

Capuchin monkey

seventeen inches (forty-three centimeters) in length – not counting their tail, which adds another eighteen inches (forty-six centimeters). The babies are well cared for by their mothers. If one should stray and get lost by chance, the other members of the group will help to get it safely home. Capuchins are lively and very intelligent.

Marmosets

Marmosets (MAHR-muh-zehts) are the smallest monkeys. Some reach only five and a half inches (fourteen centimeters) in length. There are ten species, found mostly in the region of the Amazon River in South America. Marmosets live in trees and have claws instead of nails. The tail is not prehensile.

Marmosets are good parents, with the males sharing in the care of offspring. The father assists at the birth of the infant and often carries it around on his back. At feeding time, he returns the baby to its mother. Marmosets are gentle but nervous animals. They panic easily at unexpected noises or movements.

Marmosets

Old World Monkeys

Old World monkeys are split into two groups. One includes such members as the macaques, the mangabeys, the guenons, and the baboons. These are *omnivores*, which means that they eat meat and insects as well as fruit. Many of them live on the ground. The other group includes the colobus monkeys, the langurs, and the proboscis monkeys, which are all plant-eaters. These monkeys are mainly arboreal.

Macaques

The most numerous of the Old World monkeys are the macaques (muh-KAHKS). Many of these live mainly on the ground. Some lack a tail and are incorrectly called apes. There are about a dozen species of macaques, the best known of

Rhesus monkey

Common baboon

which is the rhesus monkey. Macaques live together in large groups and are strong and courageous. They can get along well both on the ground and in trees.

Baboons

There are several species of baboons, all living in Africa. They are large monkeys, ranging from 20 inches (50 centimeters) to 40 inches (102 centimeters) in body length. They have long, doglike muzzles and live more on the ground than in the trees. Baboons live in groups, with the males guarding the females and children. They are powerful and brave fighters, even chasing off leopards when they threaten the group.

Guenons

There are twelve species of guenons (guh-NAWNs), all living in Africa. They vary in color and size, three to fifteen pounds (about one and a half to seven kilograms). Most guenons live in trees. All have round heads, slender bodies, long hind legs, and a long tail. They also have cheek pouches for holding food. Guenons live in groups, sometimes with a male leader.

Guenon

Langurs

Fruit- and leaf-eating species of langurs live throughout India and Southeast Asia. Some are found in the snow-covered evergreen forests of the Himalayas. They have slender bodies, long tails, and long, slim hands. They live high up in the trees most of the time, but do drop down to the ground to drink water or to sunbathe. On the ground, they are fast runners. In the trees, their speed is remarkable.

Apes

Apes are much larger animals than monkeys. The size of an ape's brain is also larger, making the ape's head big and round. Apes are too big to walk in the branches of trees as monkeys do. Instead, apes swing from branch to branch by using their long arms and fingers. Their hind legs are short, however, and they have no tail.

Moloch or Silvery gibbon

Face of orangutan

Apes are divided into two groups. The great apes are the largest apes. They are gorillas, orangutans, and chimpanzees. Gibbons are the smallest apes. They are called lesser apes.

Apes have a highly developed social and family life. They can make a wide variety of sounds and facial expressions. They are all extremely intelligent. Some even use tools, such as sticks, to dig out insects for food.

Gibbons

There are several species of gibbons living in Southeast Asian rain forests. They reach a length of about three feet (ninety-one centimeters). The arms of gibbons are longer and their bodies more slender than those of other apes. They are the most acrobatic of all mammals. They swing and walk through tree branches with great ease. Gibbons live in family groups. Each family has its own territory, which is guarded fiercely against other gibbons.

Orangutan

The orangutan lives only on the islands of Borneo and Sumatra. It is second in size only to the gorilla, reaching a height of about four and a half feet (almost a meter and a half). The long arms, which reach down to its ankles when it stands, are very powerful. On the ground, orangutans walk on all fours, with their knuckles touching the ground. They build sleeping nests in trees each night, using sticks and vines.

The orangutan's arms are very powerful. They can hang from trees by one arm.

Gibbons move through trees with a swinging motion.

Chimpanzee

The chimpanzee lives in the tropical rain forests and dry grasslands of Africa. It stays in groups of about twenty to forty. Chimpanzees are extremely intelligent and know how to make and use simple tools. Although they eat mostly plants, they also feed on fish, bird eggs, and ants. Chimpanzees sometimes hunt and eat baboons, red-tail monkeys, and wild hogs.

Chimpanzees live in groups.

Young chimpanzees are carefully tended by their mothers. They remain with their mothers for as long as six years. When they begin to mature, their fathers start to teach them and to play with them.

Chimpanzees spend less time in the trees than gibbons and orangutans, but are not as confident on the ground as gorillas.

Gorilla

Gorillas live in one of two places: the coastal lowlands of western Africa along the Congo River, or the mountains farther inland. Gorillas are the largest of the primates, reaching a height of almost 6 feet (1.8 meters) and weighing 450 pounds (203 kilograms). They have powerful shoulders and chests and very long arms. They walk on all fours, with their knees slightly bent, and move slowly in a stooped position, with their knuckles touching the ground.

Gorilla

Face of a gorilla baby

Gorillas are plant-eaters only. They live in bands of about ten members, with a dominant male as the leader. A band never stays in the same place for more than one night. Each evening, gorillas build a nest in the trees to sleep.

Gorillas are generally silent animals, but they can make about twenty distinct sounds, or calls. They are shy and like to avoid trouble. But if forced, they are fierce and powerful fighters.

Gorilla feeding

Edentates

There is a group of unusual animals, most of which live in South America, called *edentates* (ee-DEHN-tayts). The word *edentate* means "without teeth." Members of this order are the armadillos, the sloths, and the anteaters. The armadillos and sloths are not really toothless, but they have no front teeth and no hard layer of tooth enamel. Their molars, or grinding teeth, are located in the back of the mouth.

One of the most surprising things about these animals is the structure of their backbone. There are extra attachments between the vertebrae, which strengthen the spine and allow it to become quite rigid. No other mammal has such a backbone. The edentates are also unique in not having the standard number of neck vertebrae. In all other land mammals (including humans), there are seven, but the edentates have from six to nine neck vertebrae, depending on the species. Their feet have large, strong claws, and their brain is small and primitive.

*The pangolin –
a relative of the armadillo*

The armadillo can roll itself into a ball.

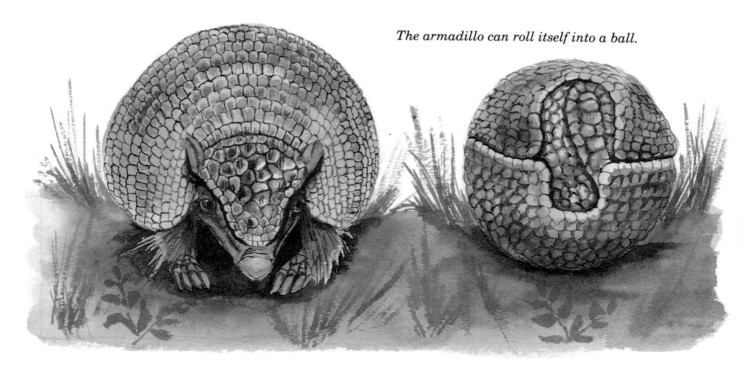

Armadillos

Armadillos, like the other edentates, at one time lived only in South America. However, one species, the nine-banded armadillo, has been moving ever northward and now also inhabits the southern parts of the United States. Armadillos can be instantly recognized by their outer coat, or armor. It is made of separate plates of bone connected by flexible skin. It covers the body, the outer part of the legs, and the top of the head. The tail is usually encased in bony rings. One type of armadillo is able to roll itself up into a ball, with its tail fitting perfectly into notches in the armor. This makes it practically impossible for an attacker to harm it. Usually, though, armadillos burrow their way to safety, using their long claws.

Armadillos range in size from five inches (about thirteen centimeters) to three and a half feet (about one meter). The armor varies in color from pink to brown. The under part of the body is covered with soft hair. The armadillo's teeth are small, numerous, and constantly growing. One species has ninety teeth.

Armadillos live in burrows when they are not active. When they do move about, they walk on the tips of the claws of their fingers and flat on the soles of their feet. The armadillo's long tongue is handy for licking up insects. Armadillos also eat earthworms, spiders, and land snails.

Several nine-banded armadillos are often found together in burrows. Usually, they are divided into all-male or all-female groups.

Giant armadillo

Sloths

In the South American forests, sloths hang upside down from the branches of trees. There are two types: the three-toed sloths and the two-toed sloths, each with several species. The size varies from about twenty inches (fifty centimeters) to about twenty-six inches (sixty-five centimeters).

Three-toed sloth

Two-toed sloth

The name *sloth* refers to the slow, lazy habits of these odd animals, which usually hang by all four feet from tree branches. When they move, they use a very slow, hand-over-hand motion. They cannot walk, but if they are on a flat surface, they dig in their claws and pull themselves forward inch by inch.

Sloths are so slow-moving that they are often covered with *algae*, the primitive plants you often see on the surface of ponds. This gives a green color to their fur. They have poorly developed hearing and sight. They depend almost completely on their sense of smell to find their way to food: tree leaves and buds.

Anteaters

South American anteaters walk on the sides of their hind feet and the knuckles of their forefeet. They have long, tubular snouts, which they use to poke into anthills and termite nests. Their long, sticky tongue reaches even farther into these insect homes, so an anteater can easily lap up its favorite prey by the hundreds.

Anteaters need no teeth, and they have none. Their claws are very large and sharp, and they are used for fighting off foes as well as for digging. There are three types of anteater: the tamandua, the silky anteater, and the giant anteater.

Giant anteaters live throughout South and Central America. They grow to a length of over three feet (almost one meter), with the bushy tail adding another two feet (just over half a meter).

The tongue, when extended, reaches more than a foot (thirty centimeters). Although they are powerful diggers, giant anteaters do not make burrows. They curl up to sleep in any quiet spot. If they are forced to fight, the large claws on their front feet make frightening weapons.

Silky anteater

Giant anteater

Lagomorphs

Rabbits and hares belong to an order called the *lagomorphs*, which also include pikas, small, compact animals with short ears. Lagomorphs have large, front gnawing teeth like those of rodents, but lagomorph teeth are arranged differently.

Pikas

Pikas, which are sometimes called rock rabbits, live at great heights in mountains in Asia, Europe, and North America. On Mount Everest, pikas have been found at a height of 17,000 feet (5,200 meters).

Arctic hare

Pikas, like all lagomorphs, are herbivores (plant-eaters), and most of them are social animals.

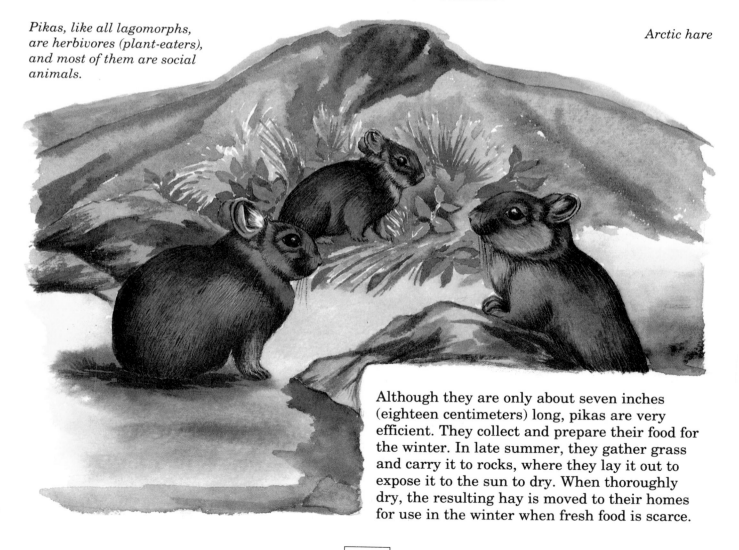

Although they are only about seven inches (eighteen centimeters) long, pikas are very efficient. They collect and prepare their food for the winter. In late summer, they gather grass and carry it to rocks, where they lay it out to expose it to the sun to dry. When thoroughly dry, the resulting hay is moved to their homes for use in the winter when fresh food is scarce.

Rabbits and Hares

Rabbits and hares are swift creatures that bound over the ground in leaps. Their hind legs are long and powerful, and their front legs are able to withstand the shock of landing. Their long ears can pick up sounds either soft or distant.

There are fifty species of rabbits and hares, which inhabit most of the world. Although they did not make it to Australia on their own, one species, the European rabbit, was brought there by people who wanted to hunt rabbits. Within a year, because there were no natural enemies, millions of them were running around eating all the vegetation. Rabbits and hares have been successful everywhere.

Although there is a difference in breeding habits between rabbits and hares, the names *rabbits* and *hares* are used so interchangeably that many of these animals are now misnamed. The jack rabbit, for instance, is really a hare. The confusion is understandable, for the differences are hard to notice. Full-grown hares are larger than adult rabbits and have longer ears, usually tipped with black. Baby rabbits, called kits or kittens, are born helpless and blind. Hare babies are much more developed when first born.

Rabbits are social animals, frequently living in large colonies, but hares are usually solitary. When rabbits are in danger, they drum with their hind feet. The sensitive ears of their burrow mates can hear the thumping sound from a long distance away.

Rabbits (left) are smaller than hares (bottom). In addition, rabbits live in underground burrows, and hares in the open.

Rodents

There are more species of rodents than all the other species of mammals combined. This group includes squirrels, beavers, gophers, rats, mice, prairie dogs, guinea pigs, lemmings, and porcupines. Rodents live in nearly every part of the world, from the hot equator to the frigid poles. Almost all rodents are small. Some only reach a length of three inches (about seven and a half centimeters). The largest of them is the capybara (kap-uh-BAHR-uh) of South America, which is about four feet (just over a meter) long. All rodents have chisel-like front teeth. They are perfectly designed for gnawing through wood and other hard objects.

The small size of rodents is one of the reasons for their success. It has allowed them to explore environments not convenient for larger animals. Their rapid rate of breeding is another important reason. Because of it, they can occupy new territory and adjust to changes in environment.

Rodent homes can be found in almost any situation. There are rodents living above ground, and there are rodents living underground in burrows. Some rodents live in trees, and some have managed to make their home in water.

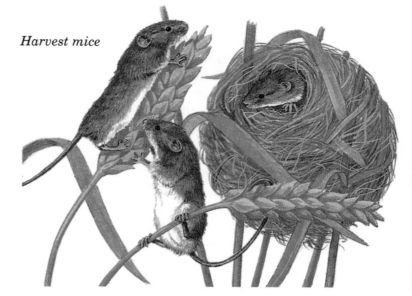

Harvest mice

Prairie dog

Rodents are great builders. In their own way, the underground burrows of prairie dogs, for instance, are as complicated as a large city. The engineering skill of beavers is excellent. Their dams, with comfortable lodges settled in the middle of the surrounding water, are wonderful structures.

European northern birch mice are recognized by the dark stripe down their backs.

The house mouse (below left) is usually found where people live. Only a few live in the wild.

Squirrels

When we say the word *squirrel*, we think about animals with fluffy tails that live in trees. But there are also ground squirrels, like chipmunks, prairie dogs, and woodchucks, that are all burrowers. Flying squirrels, which have a winglike fold of skin between the front and hind legs, are able to glide from branch to branch.

The familiar tree-dwelling squirrels live safely up in trees where food is often abundant. Most of them store food for the long winter months.

Rats and Mice

Rats and mice are the most successful rodents, with more kinds than any of the other rodent groups. There are rice rats, red-nosed rats, and climbing rats in South America; deer mice, golden mice, and grasshopper mice in North America; bamboo rats in Asia; bush rats in Africa; water rats in Australia; and dormice in Europe. These are just a few of the species in this group.

European red squirrels

summer coat

spring coat

winter coat

Gray squirrel

American harvest mouse

Porcupines

New World porcupines include a number of South American species and also the North American porcupine, which is found from the Arctic to northern Mexico. The North American porcupine lives mainly in pine forests. It is a large, heavyset rodent, which climbs well but slowly and has excellent balance. It has long, sharp quills on its body. The quills are hollow, which makes it easy for the porcupine to stay afloat when swimming.

South American porcupine

The North American porcupine eats leaves, bark, buds, and twigs. Its hearing and sense of smell are good. Porcupine quills are frightening weapons, which can cause death if they penetrate vital organs. Nevertheless, porcupines are preyed upon by many mammal carnivores as well as the great horned owl.

Prehensile-tailed porcupine

Carnivores

When the mammals took over the world, they found a great variety of food available to them. There are mammals that eat grass, those that eat leaves, insect-eaters, fish-eaters, and those that eat the flesh of other types of animals. One group became so specialized for the eating of flesh that they are called the carnivores, or flesh-eaters.

The life of a carnivore is more difficult than the life of a plant-eater. Plant-eaters can ramble around, grazing and browsing on the plants growing around them. Carnivores usually have to track down their prey, then attack and kill it in order to satisfy their appetites. To do this, they have to be faster and more intelligent than the animals they hunt. They have strong, flexible legs capable of quick movements, and their teeth are as useful in killing as they are in chewing. The carnivores' sense of smell is highly developed, and they need it to find their prey.

The open mouth of a tiger shows its sharp canine teeth.

African lion

Although there are some ways in which these animals are alike, there are also major differences. They are all descended from insectivore (insect-eating) ancestors. Wolves, tigers, bears, raccoons, weasels, and mongooses are all carnivores.

Dogs

Members of the dog family have long legs for fast running and great endurance in chasing their prey. Their teeth are sharp for slicing up meat, and their brain case is large.

The dog family includes wolves, coyotes, jackals, foxes, and wild and tamed dogs. Some members of this group can be found on every continent except Antarctica. There are dogs living on mountains and prairies as well as in deserts and jungles. Even at the North Pole and along the equator, dogs have been able to survive.

Although all dogs have certain traits in common, they come in a wide range of sizes and shapes. The little desert fox, or fennec, is only fourteen inches (about thirty-six centimeters) long, while the timber wolf measures four and a half feet (about a meter and a half). Dogs are alert animals, active night and day. Even in the coldest places, they hunt throughout the winter. They all have good hearing and sight, although they hunt mainly by scent. They usually catch their prey by chasing them down.

Timber wolf

One breed of tamed dog – the hard-working St. Bernard.

Some members of the dog family, such as wolves, live in large packs and usually hunt in relays, stationing members of the pack at given places along their planned route to take turns in the chase. Others, such as coyotes and jackals, hunt singly or in pairs. Foxes hunt alone and also live alone, except to mate.

Fennec

Foxes

There are nine species of foxes that live in North America, Europe, Africa, and Asia. They have large, pointed ears, a long muzzle, and a bushy tail. Foxes feed mainly on rodents.

Wolves and Coyotes

A number of scientists believe there are two species of wolf: the gray wolf and the red wolf. Most wolves, in fact, belong to the gray wolf species, which includes timber wolves and tundra wolves. Timber wolves live in wooded regions below the Arctic. Tundra wolves live on the Arctic plains themselves. (A tundra is a huge, treeless, polar plain.) Wolves in general are intelligent and social animals, living and hunting in packs.

At one time, the gray wolf species was widely spread throughout North America, Europe, and Asia. But now it lives only where there are few people. The red wolf species is close to extinction, with the few still alive found mostly in captivity. Once, they were found throughout the south-central United States.

Red fox

Fox tracks

Gray wolf

While the wolves have become more restricted in their range, the coyotes of North America have extended their territory considerably. They can now be found from Alaska to Central America.

Coyotes run at speeds up to forty miles (sixty-four kilometers) an hour and can track down such fast prey as jack rabbits and rodents. Coyotes usually hunt singly rather than in packs.

Wild Dogs

Among the dogs that live in the wild are the dingoes of Australia and the hunting dogs of Africa. Rusty yellow in color with irregular white markings, dingoes are less than five feet (one and a half meters) long. They live and hunt in packs, like wolves, and prey on kangaroos and sheep. Many scientists think dingoes are descended from an ancient wolf.

African hunting dogs are 30-40 inches (75-100 centimeters) long, with a dark coat that has yellow and white blotches on it. These wild dogs can run at a fast speed over a three-mile (five kilometer) stretch. They hunt in packs, often catching and killing gazelles and zebras.

Jackals

There are three species of jackals that live in the Middle East, Asia, and Africa. Jackals move singly or in small groups, usually following the big cats to feed on what they leave after a kill. On their own, jackals hunt small mammals and insects.

Jackal

Jackals live in family groups.

Bears

Early in the history of dogs, one line of large dogs took on certain distinct traits. They developed a huge skull, wide teeth, and short, heavy legs and feet. The tail was no more than a stub. This line of dogs became big, heavy carnivores – bears.

Seven species of bears now live in the Northern Hemisphere and the northern part of South America. The Alaskan brown bear is the largest of all the carnivores. It reaches a length of 9 feet (2.7 meters) and weighs up to 1,700 pounds (770 kilograms). It belongs to the same species that includes grizzly bears and Old World brown bears.

Polar bears live in the same Arctic regions as seals, walruses, and other sea animals. Polar bears wander for great distances and drift for hundreds of miles on ice floes (masses or sheets of floating ice). They can outrun a reindeer and swim almost as well as the seals they prey on. Polar bears often fight with walruses, whose long, sharp canine teeth make the polar bears frequent losers.

Grizzly bear

Polar bear

Raccoons and Pandas

Raccoons and pandas are closely related to dogs and descended from the same ancestors. They belong to the same family as ring-tailed cats (which are not true cats), coatis, and kinkajous. These animals all have teeth suited for eating both plant matter and meat.

Raccoon

Raccoons live from Canada to South America. They eat many types of food, including the contents of outside garbage pails, although they are fussy about washing their food in a stream or a puddle of water before eating it.

There are two kinds of pandas. One is the lesser panda, also called the red panda, which lives only in the Himalayan mountains. With its ringed tail and masked eyes, the lesser panda looks very much like a raccoon. The other kind

Giant pandas

of panda is the giant panda. This large, black-and-white animal looks more like a bear. Giant pandas used to wander throughout Asia, but they now live only in western China. They are carnivores that prefer to eat plants. Their molar teeth are low and blunt, suitable for crunching green bamboo shoots, which are their main food. A giant panda will also eat an occasional rodent or fish. Some scientists place the giant panda in its own separate family among carnivores.

Weasels, Skunks, and Otters

Another group stemming from the doglike carnivores has developed in a different manner. This group includes such animals as weasels, badgers, skunks, wolverines, and otters. These animals range in size from the least weasel, just ten inches (twenty-five centimeters) long, to the giant otter, which reaches seven feet (two meters) in length. Besides the differences in size, there are many different ways of life among these animals.

The weasels, martens, and minks are fierce, bloodthirsty hunters, sometimes killing for no reason at all. These are the smallest members of the family. The wolverines, although larger, are closely related to the weasel group. Wolverines specialize in eating carrion (the meat of dead animals).

Skunks will eat almost anything, from plant matter to insects, rodents, and rattlesnakes. They live in the woods, plains, and deserts of North and South America, where their defensive, smelly glandular secretions make them feared by all.

Wolverine and tracks

River otters are water-going carnivores. They feed mostly on fish, but frogs, turtles, and geese are also acceptable food. The sea otter likes shellfish. It floats along on its back, placing sea urchins or abalone shells on its chest and hammering them open with a rock.

Otter

Cats

While some carnivores eventually turned into dogs, others developed different characteristics and eventually turned into cats. These animals have a small, round head set on a short neck; a muscular and flexible body; strong, heavy legs; and efficient teeth. Every part of a cat's body is designed for hunting and killing other animals. The flexibility of the cat's skeleton and the strength of the legs allow for its quick spring and pounce. The long, sharp claws are carried in sheaths when not in use, which prevents breaking. The cat's teeth are used for stabbing and slicing. The short, heavy neck absorbs the severe shock caused by the violent actions of the head and teeth.

The cat family includes the large cats – pumas, jaguars, leopards, tigers, lions, and cheetahs – and numerous small- and medium-sized species, including the ancestors of tamed cats. They cannot be found in Antarctica or Australia but are plentiful on every other continent. Aside from differences in size and color pattern, the members of this group resemble each other closely. Their most striking trait is their hunting ability – from the tamed or domestic cats' pursuit of house mice to the Bengal tigers' stalking of water buffaloes.

Black-coated leopard (black panther)

Tamed cats are popular pets.

Unlike dogs, cats are solitary hunters, although some of them do live in groups. Lions, for instance, form prides (groups) of as many as twenty-five members.

Seals, Sea Lions, and Walruses

The *pinnipeds*, which include seals, sea lions, and walruses, are also descendants of the early carnivores. They developed special adaptations to allow them to live much of their lives in the sea. They have paddlelike legs that help them swim, and their toes are webbed. Sea lions and walruses are able to turn their back legs forward or backward, allowing them to move along freely on the ground. Seals have permanently fixed back paddles and have to squiggle along on their bellies when they are on land.

Gray seal and pup

Elephant seal

Seal and sea-lion teeth are excellent for catching fish. Walruses have large tusks, which they use for digging up the clams they feed on. Sea lions (sometimes called "eared seals") have small, external ears, but walruses and seals have none.

Sea lions live in the Pacific, South Atlantic, and Indian oceans. Some of them, such as the fur seals, have beautiful, thick fur. Many of them travel north and gather together on the islands in the cold Bering Sea each year for breeding. After the young have matured somewhat, they all travel south, returning to warmer waters.

Walruses live in the cold, open waters of the Arctic, North Atlantic, and North Pacific oceans. They migrate south to avoid the ice and return north as soon as it melts. Walruses have fat bodies with round heads, short necks, and large tusks. Their skin is tough and wrinkled. Big bulls (the males) can be as much as 12 feet (3.7 meters) long and weigh up to 2,500 pounds (1,100 kilograms). Cows (the females) are smaller. Both males and females have tusks, but the males' grow larger, up to three and a half feet (one meter) long. All walruses, even babies, have thick, bristly mustaches.

Walruses live in herds. They bellow loudly whenever any stranger approaches, and they will attack an invader. Calves (the young) nurse for as long as two years and travel about on their mothers' necks.

Seals are the most abundant of the pinnipeds. They can be found in all the oceans of the world as well as in several freshwater lakes. There are thirteen types of seals, ranging in size from the four foot (about one meter) long ringed seal to the twenty foot (six meter) long elephant seal.

Seals do not come together in huge colonies. They travel alone or in small groups. They frequently swim on their backs.

Hoofed Animals

Plant-eaters that have hoofs on their feet are called *ungulates* (UN-gya-lits), a general term that includes a number of different groups.

Ungulates are plant-eaters that have teeth specially designed for chewing vegetable matter. Their digestive tract, where food is turned into a simple form the body can use, is specialized for plant-eating. Ungulates have long legs and feet, with toes ending in hoofs that cushion the shock of running over hard ground. Many of them have antlers or horns for use in mating displays or combat.

Walruses have enormous tusks. They were once hunted for their ivory.

A female (left) and a male red deer.
A female deer is called a doe.

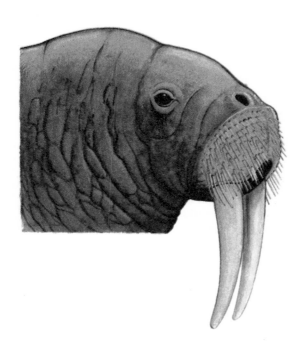

Odd-Toed Hoofed Animals

Horses belong to a group of odd-toed hoofed animals. This group also includes tapirs and rhinoceroses. Although there do not seem to be many similarities between a horse and a rhinoceros, they do share some traits. The number of toes on each foot is usually odd: one, three, or five. The animal's weight is carried mainly on the central toe.

Mountain zebra

Horse

Horses

The horse family includes horses, zebras, and donkeys. Several species of zebra live in Africa, and there are several kinds of wild donkeys in Asia and Africa. All are greatly reduced in number. Only one species of wild horse, the Mongolian wild horse, survives in central Asia.

Domestic horses, bred from wild ancestors and now numbering over 150 different breeds, are used worldwide. Mustangs are not true wild horses. They are descended from domestic horses brought to North America by the Spanish explorers.

Rhinoceroses

Like the wild horses, the rhinoceroses (or rhinos) are also in danger of becoming extinct. There are just a few of each of the five species still alive. Rhinoceroses are bulky, heavyset animals with three toes on each foot. Their unique horns are not made of bone, but are formed of keratin, the same substance that human nails are made of. Rhinoceroses live in Africa and Asia.

The black rhinoceros of Africa has been hunted for so long that there are not very many left. The African white rhino and the Asian two-horned rhino are now protected by law, but they are so close to extinction that they probably cannot be saved. The one-horned rhinoceros of Java has been reduced to only fifty survivors. In India, the giant one-horned rhino, twelve feet (almost four meters) long and with a skin like a suit of metal armor, has been almost completely killed off.

Rhinoceroses have tiny, shortsighted eyes and poor intelligence.

The American bighorn is a kind of mountain goat. The males, or rams, have splendid horns.

African black rhinoceros

Even-Toed Hoofed Animals

The even-toed ungulates are a larger and more varied order than the odd-toed hoofed animals. Some living animals of the group are pigs, hippopotamuses, camels, deer, antelopes, cattle, goats, and sheep. There seems to be a large difference between a dainty deer and a mud-wallowing hippopotamus, yet they share a similar body structure.

Members of this group have an even number of toes on each foot, either two or four. The most important thing is that their weight is carried between the two middle toes. Their teeth are different from those of the odd-toed animals. Some have knifelike canine teeth for fighting.

Pigs and Peccaries

Pigs and peccaries developed at the same time – the pigs in Europe and the peccaries in North America. Pigs are considerably larger than peccaries. Their skulls are longer and their canine teeth are large, outwardly curved tusks. Peccaries rely more on running than fighting, so they have longer legs. A large gland on their back releases a strong odor, called musk, when they are excited.

Peccaries live in the southern part of the United States and in Mexico, Central America, and South America. Several species of wild pigs can be found in Europe, Africa, and Asia. The European wild hog is the ancestor of all the domestic breeds of pig. Some wild pigs, such as the African wart hog and the babirusa of Indonesia, are strange-looking because of the odd tusk formations that appear in the males. The tusks function as decorative ornaments as well as weapons.

Wart hog

Hippopotamuses

Hippopotamuses, or hippos, are the only aquatic (water-dwelling) even-toed ungulates. When they are submerged, hippopotamuses have small, protruding eyes set on top of the skull for ease in seeing. Their nostrils are located on top of the snout and can be closed. Hippopotamuses have special pores in their skin that secrete a pink substance called "blood sweat," which is thick and oily. This fluid stops the animal's skin from drying out. The odd-looking teeth are ideal for eating water plants.

There are two species of hippopotamuses. One species, the river hippopotamus, includes the large hippos living in all rivers and streams of Africa. They can get as long as fifteen feet (about five meters) and weigh up to five tons (four and a half metric tons). The pygmy hippos, which live only in Liberia, form the other species. They are only 5 feet (1½ meters) long and weigh about 400 pounds (180 kilograms).

Hippopotamuses like to wallow in mud to keep cool.

Ruminants

Ruminant is a name applied to a large group of even-toed ungulates that include deer, giraffes, and cattle and that chew the cud. This refers to the complex digestive system necessary for the large volume of food these animals require. There are four compartments in the stomach through which the food passes before reaching the intestines. The first and largest of the compartments is called a *rumen*. It is a storehouse for food quickly swallowed. This food is brought

Common eland

Camels

up again after being softened in the rumen. Then it is thoroughly chewed and swallowed again for digestion in the other compartments of the stomach.

All the ruminants have excellent eyesight and long ears to assist in hearing. Most of them have horns or antlers.

Deer antlers grow from horny knobs in the skull and are shed each year when they are developed to their fullest extent.

The cud-chewing digestive ability of camels is not as well developed as it is in deer, antelopes, and cattle. The stomachs of camels have only three compartments. Camels are two-toed ungulates. They have long legs for fast running. They also have long necks. The South American llamas are placed in the same family with camels, but llamas do not have the camels' distinct humps.

Camels live in the deserts of Africa and Asia. The humps store fat, so that camels do not need to eat as often as some other animals. Their eyes have long lashes, their ears are hairy, and their nostrils are closable. These all serve as protective measures against sandstorms.

Camel

Deer

What sets deer apart from the other even-toed hoofed animals is their antlers. Antlers are bones that grow from the skull above the eyes. Two bony stumps serve as bases from which new, skin-covered antlers grow each year. When the antlers reach full size, the skin, called velvet, dries and the deer rubs it off against trees. In most species, only the males have antlers. Male deer use their new hard spikes while fighting each other during the mating season. At the end of the season, the antlers fall off and begin to form all over again the next year.

Various species of deer live in North America, Central and South America, Europe, and Asia. North American deer include white-tailed deer, mule deer, elk, and moose. Deer eat many types of plants, grasses, twigs, and stems.

Giraffes

You can tell from looking at a giraffe that it lives on a diet of leaves and fruit found high up in trees. The long legs and extra-long neck of a giraffe give it an advantage in getting this food.

Giraffes live throughout Africa, wherever acacia (uh-KAY-shuh) trees grow. Like most mammals, the giraffe has only seven neck vertebrae, but these are very long. With its long neck and stiltlike legs, a giraffe can stand seventeen feet (over five meters) tall.

Giraffes

Cattle and Their Relatives

Cattle, antelopes, buffaloes, bison, sheep, and goats all belong to the same family of even-toed hoofed animals. They all have powerful bodies and long legs. They have teeth specially adapted to eating hard grasses. Permanent horns are usually worn by both sexes. These animals live in North America, Asia, Europe, and Africa.

The best known of the North American species is the bison, which at one time wandered in enormous herds across the western prairies. So many of them were killed by hunters in the 1800s that they were almost extinct before conservation laws were passed to protect the few remaining herds.

There are seven wild species of true cattle. Domestic cattle were probably descended from a species of wild cattle with long horns, called *aurochs*, which are now extinct. In Tibet, the domestic yak has been of great value. In India, domestic cattle are all varieties of zebu, which have been interbred with European stock.

Water buffalo

Antelope

Elephants

Elephants don't quite fit in as hoofed mammals. Most of their foot rests on a padding of fat, and they have toes with nails instead of hoofs. Although there are only two species living today (one in Africa and one in Asia) there were once many different kinds roaming the earth. You may have heard about the mastodons and mammoths that lived in North America, Europe, and Asia. Mammoths were especially hunted by early man.

The two elephant species resemble each other, but they can be distinguished by several characteristics. The African elephant is larger, reaching a height of eleven feet (almost three and a half meters), while the Indian elephant never gets much over ten feet (three meters).

African elephants have big, fanlike ears, while Indian elephant ears are smaller and closer to the head. The African elephant's head slopes back, while the Indian elephant's is domed. At the end of the trunk of the African elephant, there are two small, flexible lobes used for picking up food. The Indian elephant species has just one lobe at the end of its trunk.

Elephants are social animals, living in large herds. The leaders are usually females. If one member of the herd is wounded, the others will assist it in its efforts to reach safety. When a female is ready to give birth, the whole herd stops and waits until the baby is strong enough to travel with the group.

African elephants live in family groups.

Whales

At one time, all life was in the sea. The land was barren. It took millions of years for animals to get to the point where they could live on land. The problems of such a change were enormous. Movement on solid ground requires a totally different body structure from that required for life in the water. Getting oxygen from the air instead of from the water involves other changes. Reproduction on land is different from reproduction in the sea. Among vertebrates, the early amphibians adapted to all the new conditions, with the exception of reproduction. From that point on, the dramatic changes were those of egg-laying or live-bearing land dwellers. Vertebrates became well adapted to their new environment.

Yet the call of the sea has been very strong. In each major group of land vertebrates, one or more species returned to the sea. The move back to the sea has been no easier than the one toward land. All the body changes made for land living had to be modified, or changed again. The problems of movement, breathing, and reproduction had to be overcome in reverse.

Of the mammals who made this change, the one that has been most modified is the whale. The ancestry of this creature is still mysterious. There are things about the skull that seem to relate it to the early carnivores.

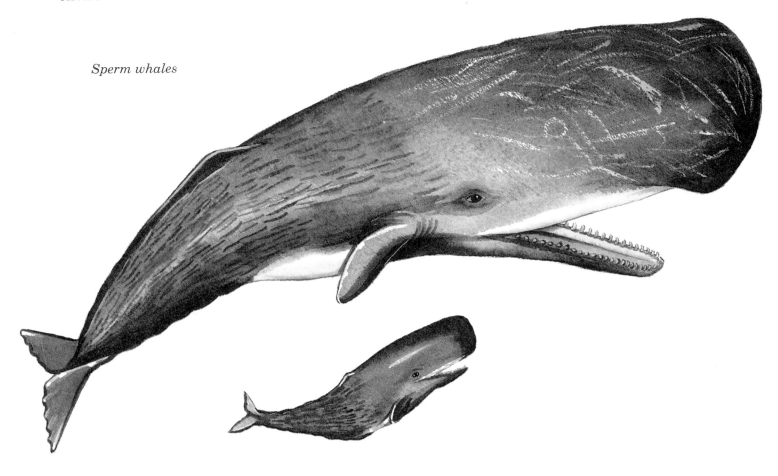

Sperm whales

Whatever their origin, whales developed rapidly into aquatic animals. They developed a body much like that of the fishes – streamlined and torpedo-shaped with no neck. They became smooth-skinned rather than hairy, making a sleek surface for gliding through the water. Whales also developed a thick layer of blubber (body fat) under the skin for insulating their warm-blooded bodies.

The backbone became flexible, with long muscles running to the tail, to propel the whales through the water. The tail ends in horizontal fins, called flukes, that move up and down. This is unique to aquatic mammals. Other vertebrates that live in the water have vertical tail fins that move from side to side.

The front legs of these mammals have been changed into paddles, with the arm and wrist bones flattened and the fingers made longer. The hind legs are little stumps hidden in the body. Modern whales have their nostrils up on top of the skull, forming a blowhole. What is spouted out of the blowhole is not water but vapor from the air exhaled, or breathed out, from the lungs. The lungs, which stretch, can take in a lot of air. For this reason, some whales can remain underwater for as long as an hour.

Whales can hear very well in the water, and they can detect sounds outside the human range of hearing. They have very poor eyesight and no sense of smell. The brain is very well developed, and they are extremely intelligent. Whales live in complex social groups, calling to each other over long distances. The sounds, called phonations, have been studied by scientists. The sounds are varied and seem to be a complex form of communication.

The blue whale is the biggest animal in the world.

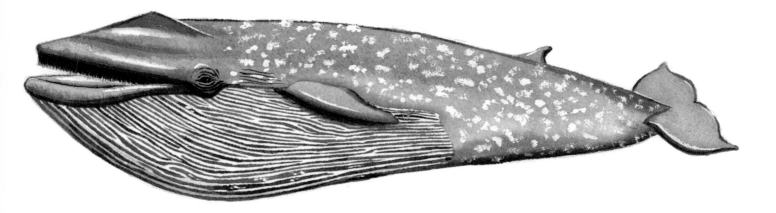

All whales are carnivorous. They are divided into two groups. Toothed whales have teeth and eat fish and other marine creatures. Dolphins are small-toothed whales. The other group, called baleen whales, do not have teeth. Instead, they have baleen (plates of hardened skin) in their mouths for filtering tiny animals and plants from the water.

The solution to the problem of reproduction has been to bear very large, well-developed young capable of swimming along with the mother. The mammary glands are protected by a fold of skin that resembles a pocket, so the baby can nurse while submerged.

There are about seventy-five species of whales and dolphins. They live in all the seas of the world and in some rivers and lakes. The largest of them all – in fact, the largest mammal that has ever lived – is the blue whale, which can measure as much as 100 feet (30 meters) long and weigh up to 300 tons (136 metric tons).

Whitefin dolphin

Killer whale

Animals and People

From the first, people have admired, used, and abused the animals around them. Early man hunted other animals as food. It was not long before humans formed relationships with wild dogs to assist the humans in their hunting and to guard their homes while they slept. These wild dogs were probably grateful for the constant supply of food they received in return for their efforts. As the early humans moved about looking for fresh supplies of meat, they brought their dogs with them. These dogs bred with wild dogs of related species who were nearby. The domestic dog was the first in a long line of domestic animals.

About 10,000 years ago in Asia, North Africa, and Europe, people settled down to farm, instead of being always on the move while hunting. As a result, they looked for more constant supplies of meat. Goats and sheep were then tamed as easily available meat animals. Sheep had an additional advantage in that their wool could be clipped for use in making clothing.

Cattle were probably bred from a single ancestor, the aurochs. The aurochs were long-horned animals still around in the time of Julius Caesar (100-44 B.C.). He wrote about the aurochs, which could then be found in the forests of North Africa, Europe, and southwestern Asia. They became extinct about 1627. There are now many different breeds of cattle serving people. Some are used primarily for their milk, while others are raised for the meat they provide.

Highland cow

Cheetah tamed by Egyptians

Pigs were tamed from wild hogs, which are found in Europe, Africa, and Asia. In the few areas where there are still wild bands of them wandering through the countryside, they are now hunted for sport.

In the early farming communities, people noticed that cats were excellent rodent killers. They brought the cats into their homes and granaries to rid them of the little invaders. Small, wild cats of different species were tamed in various parts of the world. As people and their cats moved around, the various strains of domestic cat interbred. Cats became so well mixed that it is impossible to distinguish any one ancestor. By 1300 B.C., cats were so important to Egyptians that they were worshipped.

Horses have been extremely valuable to humans for their use as riding or pack animals. Through selective breeding and taming, many breeds of horses have been developed. There is only one species of wild horse surviving in the world today, and that is in the Altai Mountains of Mongolia. Even these horses have been almost totally wiped out by people.

Chickens are descended from the jungle fowl of Asia. We use the many different breeds that exist today for eggs and meat. American Indians tamed the wild turkey, which is now bred worldwide. Several kinds of ducks and geese were tamed in various parts of the Old World, and there are now many varieties.

Fish have always been a source of protein for people. Although we rarely raise fish on farms, a number of catfish and carp farms are now operating. And the idea of keeping other fish enclosed and readily available is becoming more popular.

Taming did not remove the threat of human hunters on wild animals. Most are now killed for reasons other than their value as a source of meat.

Horses have done work for people for hundreds of years. Here are three breeds of tamed horse:

Suffolk punch

Clydesdale

Cleveland bay

Reptiles are rarely eaten by people, but the skins of snakes, lizards, and alligators have become popular leather products. Millions of these animals are killed for their skins every year. Others, such as rattlesnakes, are also killed because people are afraid of them. Sometimes, nonpoisonous snakes are killed because people do not know whether or not they are dangerous.

Mammals killed for their furs include various members of the weasel family, beavers, foxes, leopards, raccoons, and sea lions. Many of these mammals are in danger of being wiped out.

People kill animals for various other reasons. Some animals, such as the endangered rhinoceroses, are hunted for their horns, which are ground up as medicine in some countries. Whales are hunted for the oil their bodies contain. Other animals are often wrongly considered a threat to humans' meat supplies. These include wolves, coyotes, and bears. Still other animals are killed for sport by people.

Beaver – hunted for its fur

Harp seal pup

Now all wild animals, whether they are hunted or not, are facing a new problem caused by humanity: the lack of room on earth. In our efforts to provide homes and food for the people of the earth, we have taken much of the land that was once used by animals. We have often turned wilderness areas into places suitable for ourselves and our tamed animals – without leaving much for those animals still wild.

The earth belongs to all living things – wild animals, tamed animals, us. And it is mostly up to us to share the earth with other creatures in a more responsible, caring way.